50 Festive Desserts for Every Holiday

By: Kelly Johnson

Table of Contents

- Gingerbread Cookies
- Pumpkin Pie
- Eggnog Cheesecake
- Cranberry Orange Bread
- Yule Log Cake
- Sugar Cookies with Royal Icing
- Chocolate Truffles
- Apple Crisp
- Pecan Pie
- Carrot Cake with Cream Cheese Frosting
- Chocolate Mousse
- Cinnamon Rolls
- Lemon Bars
- Peppermint Bark
- Fruitcake
- Molasses Cookies
- Cherry Clafoutis
- Chocolate-Dipped Strawberries
- Raisin Pudding Cake
- Tiramisu
- Coconut Cream Pie
- Pavlova with Berries
- Baked Alaska
- Red Velvet Cake
- Marzipan Cookies
- Ricotta Cheesecake
- Sweet Potato Pie
- S'mores Brownies
- Fudge (Chocolate, Peanut Butter, or Maple)
- Meringue Kisses
- Peach Cobbler
- Black Forest Cake
- Banoffee Pie
- Chocolate Fondue
- Fruit Sorbet

- Churros with Chocolate Sauce
- Cranberry Cheesecake Bars
- Chocolate-Covered Pretzels
- Key Lime Pie
- Rugelach
- Baked Apple Dumplings
- Cinnamon Sugar Donuts
- Sticky Toffee Pudding
- Chocolate Lava Cakes
- Lemon Meringue Pie
- Almond Biscotti
- Chantilly Cream-Filled Profiteroles
- Berry Crumble
- Chocolate-Coconut Macaroons
- Peach Melba

Gingerbread Cookies

Ingredients:

- 3 1/4 cups all-purpose flour
- 1 teaspoon baking soda
- 2 teaspoons ground ginger
- 1 teaspoon ground cinnamon
- 1/2 teaspoon ground cloves
- 1/2 teaspoon ground nutmeg
- 1/2 teaspoon salt
- 3/4 cup unsalted butter, softened
- 3/4 cup dark brown sugar
- 1 large egg
- 1/2 cup molasses
- 1 teaspoon vanilla extract

Instructions:

1. **Preheat the Oven**:
   Preheat your oven to 350°F (175°C) and line baking sheets with parchment paper.
2. **Prepare the Dough**:
   In a medium bowl, whisk together the flour, baking soda, and spices. In a separate bowl, beat the butter and brown sugar until creamy. Add the egg, molasses, and vanilla, mixing until smooth. Gradually add the dry ingredients and mix until the dough comes together. Divide the dough in half, wrap in plastic wrap, and chill for at least 30 minutes.
3. **Roll and Cut the Dough**:
   Roll the dough out on a floured surface to about 1/4-inch thickness. Cut into desired shapes (gingerbread men, stars, etc.).
4. **Bake**:
   Place the cookies on the prepared baking sheets and bake for 8-10 minutes, or until firm. Allow to cool completely before decorating.
5. **Decorate**:
   Once cooled, decorate with royal icing or colored sugar if desired.

Pumpkin Pie

Ingredients:

- 1 pie crust (store-bought or homemade)
- 2 cups pumpkin puree
- 1 cup heavy cream
- 3/4 cup granulated sugar
- 2 large eggs
- 1 teaspoon ground cinnamon
- 1/2 teaspoon ground ginger
- 1/4 teaspoon ground nutmeg
- 1/4 teaspoon ground cloves
- 1/2 teaspoon salt

Instructions:

1. **Preheat the Oven**:
   Preheat the oven to 425°F (220°C).
2. **Prepare the Filling**:
   In a bowl, mix the pumpkin puree, heavy cream, eggs, sugar, cinnamon, ginger, nutmeg, cloves, and salt until smooth.
3. **Assemble the Pie**:
   Pour the pumpkin mixture into the pie crust.
4. **Bake the Pie**:
   Bake for 15 minutes, then reduce the temperature to 350°F (175°C) and bake for an additional 45 minutes, or until the filling is set.
5. **Cool**:
   Allow the pie to cool before serving. Optionally, top with whipped cream.

Eggnog Cheesecake

Ingredients for the Crust:

- 1 1/2 cups graham cracker crumbs
- 1/4 cup granulated sugar
- 1/2 cup unsalted butter, melted

Ingredients for the Filling:

- 3 (8 oz) packages cream cheese, softened
- 1 cup granulated sugar
- 3 large eggs
- 1/2 cup eggnog
- 1 teaspoon vanilla extract
- 1/4 teaspoon ground nutmeg
- 1/4 teaspoon ground cinnamon

Instructions:

1. **Prepare the Crust**:
   Preheat the oven to 325°F (160°C). Mix the graham cracker crumbs, sugar, and melted butter, then press the mixture into the bottom of a springform pan. Bake for 10 minutes and allow to cool.
2. **Prepare the Filling**:
   Beat the cream cheese and sugar until smooth. Add the eggs one at a time, mixing well after each. Stir in the eggnog, vanilla extract, nutmeg, and cinnamon.
3. **Bake**:
   Pour the filling into the cooled crust and bake for 55-60 minutes, or until the center is set. Let it cool in the oven with the door slightly ajar for 1 hour, then refrigerate for at least 4 hours.
4. **Serve**:
   Serve chilled, optionally garnished with whipped cream and a sprinkle of cinnamon.

Cranberry Orange Bread

Ingredients:

- 2 cups all-purpose flour
- 1 1/2 teaspoons baking powder
- 1/2 teaspoon baking soda
- 1/2 teaspoon salt
- 1 teaspoon orange zest
- 1 cup fresh cranberries (or frozen)
- 1/2 cup granulated sugar
- 1/4 cup orange juice
- 2 large eggs
- 1/2 cup unsalted butter, melted
- 1 teaspoon vanilla extract
- 1/2 cup buttermilk

Instructions:

1. **Preheat the Oven**:
   Preheat your oven to 350°F (175°C). Grease and flour a 9x5-inch loaf pan.
2. **Prepare the Dry Ingredients**:
   Whisk together the flour, baking powder, baking soda, salt, and orange zest.
3. **Prepare the Wet Ingredients**:
   Mix the sugar, orange juice, eggs, melted butter, vanilla extract, and buttermilk in another bowl.
4. **Combine**:
   Add the wet ingredients to the dry ingredients and stir until just combined. Gently fold in the cranberries.
5. **Bake**:
   Pour the batter into the loaf pan and bake for 50-60 minutes, or until a toothpick comes out clean. Cool before slicing.

Yule Log Cake

Ingredients for the Cake:

- 1/2 cup all-purpose flour
- 1/4 cup unsweetened cocoa powder
- 1 teaspoon baking powder
- 1/4 teaspoon salt
- 4 large eggs
- 1 cup granulated sugar
- 1 teaspoon vanilla extract
- 1/4 cup water

Ingredients for the Filling:

- 1 cup heavy cream
- 2 tablespoons powdered sugar
- 1 teaspoon vanilla extract

Ingredients for the Frosting:

- 1/2 cup unsalted butter, softened
- 2 cups powdered sugar
- 1/4 cup unsweetened cocoa powder
- 1/4 cup heavy cream
- 1 teaspoon vanilla extract

Instructions:

1. **Preheat the Oven:**
   Preheat the oven to 350°F (175°C). Line a 15x10-inch baking sheet with parchment paper.
2. **Make the Cake:**
   In a bowl, sift together the flour, cocoa powder, baking powder, and salt. In a separate bowl, beat the eggs and sugar until light and fluffy. Stir in the vanilla extract and water. Fold in the dry ingredients.
3. **Bake the Cake:**
   Spread the batter evenly on the prepared baking sheet. Bake for 12-15 minutes. Let it cool slightly, then roll the cake in a clean towel and chill.
4. **Prepare the Filling:**
   Whip the heavy cream with powdered sugar and vanilla until stiff peaks form.

5. **Assemble the Yule Log**:
   Unroll the cake, spread with whipped cream, and roll it back up. Frost the entire log with chocolate frosting.

Sugar Cookies with Royal Icing

Ingredients for the Cookies:

- 2 3/4 cups all-purpose flour
- 1 teaspoon baking powder
- 1 cup unsalted butter, softened
- 1 1/2 cups granulated sugar
- 1 large egg
- 1 teaspoon vanilla extract
- 1/2 teaspoon almond extract (optional)

Ingredients for the Royal Icing:

- 3 cups powdered sugar
- 2 tablespoons meringue powder
- 5-6 tablespoons water
- Food coloring (optional)

Instructions:

1. **Prepare the Cookies**:
   Preheat the oven to 350°F (175°C). In a bowl, mix the flour and baking powder. In another bowl, beat the butter and sugar until fluffy, then add the egg and extracts. Gradually add the dry ingredients and mix until smooth.
2. **Shape and Bake**:
   Roll out the dough and cut into shapes. Place on baking sheets and bake for 8-10 minutes. Let the cookies cool completely.
3. **Make the Royal Icing**:
   Beat the powdered sugar, meringue powder, and water until stiff peaks form. Color with food coloring if desired.
4. **Decorate**:
   Use the royal icing to decorate the cooled cookies.

Chocolate Truffles

Ingredients:

- 8 oz semisweet chocolate, chopped
- 1/2 cup heavy cream
- 1 teaspoon vanilla extract
- Cocoa powder, melted chocolate, or crushed nuts for coating

Instructions:

1. **Prepare the Truffle Filling**:
   Heat the heavy cream in a saucepan until it just begins to simmer. Pour over the chopped chocolate and let it sit for 5 minutes. Stir until smooth and add vanilla extract.
2. **Chill**:
   Refrigerate the mixture for about 2 hours until firm enough to scoop.
3. **Form Truffles**:
   Scoop the mixture into small balls and roll in cocoa powder, melted chocolate, or crushed nuts. Chill until set.

Apple Crisp

Ingredients:

- 6 cups apples, peeled and sliced
- 1 tablespoon lemon juice
- 1 cup rolled oats
- 1/2 cup flour
- 1/2 cup brown sugar
- 1/4 cup granulated sugar
- 1/2 teaspoon cinnamon
- 1/4 teaspoon nutmeg
- 1/4 cup unsalted butter, melted

Instructions:

1. **Prepare the Apples**:
   Toss the sliced apples with lemon juice and place them in a greased baking dish.
2. **Make the Topping**:
   In a bowl, combine the oats, flour, sugars, cinnamon, and nutmeg. Stir in the melted butter.
3. **Assemble and Bake**:
   Spread the topping over the apples. Bake at 350°F (175°C) for 40-45 minutes, or until golden brown and bubbly.

Pecan Pie

Ingredients:

- 1 pie crust
- 1 cup corn syrup
- 1 cup brown sugar
- 1/2 teaspoon vanilla extract
- 1/4 teaspoon salt
- 3 large eggs
- 1 1/2 cups pecans

Instructions:

1. **Prepare the Filling**:
   In a bowl, whisk together the corn syrup, brown sugar, vanilla, salt, and eggs.
2. **Assemble the Pie**:
   Pour the filling into the prepared pie crust and top with the pecans.
3. **Bake**:
   Bake at 350°F (175°C) for 45-50 minutes or until the filling is set and slightly puffed.

Carrot Cake with Cream Cheese Frosting

Ingredients for the Cake:

- 2 cups all-purpose flour
- 2 teaspoons baking powder
- 1 1/2 teaspoons baking soda
- 1 teaspoon ground cinnamon
- 1/2 teaspoon ground nutmeg
- 1/4 teaspoon salt
- 4 large eggs
- 1 1/2 cups granulated sugar
- 1 cup vegetable oil
- 2 teaspoons vanilla extract
- 2 cups finely grated carrots
- 1/2 cup chopped walnuts (optional)

Ingredients for the Cream Cheese Frosting:

- 8 oz cream cheese, softened
- 1/2 cup unsalted butter, softened
- 4 cups powdered sugar
- 1 teaspoon vanilla extract

Instructions:

1. **Preheat the Oven**:
   Preheat your oven to 350°F (175°C). Grease and flour two 9-inch round cake pans.
2. **Make the Cake**:
   In a large bowl, whisk together the flour, baking powder, baking soda, cinnamon, nutmeg, and salt. In another bowl, beat the eggs, sugar, oil, and vanilla extract until smooth. Stir in the grated carrots and optional walnuts. Gradually add the dry ingredients to the wet ingredients and mix until combined.
3. **Bake the Cake**:
   Divide the batter evenly between the prepared cake pans. Bake for 25-30 minutes, or until a toothpick comes out clean. Allow the cakes to cool completely.
4. **Make the Frosting**:
   Beat the cream cheese and butter until smooth and creamy. Gradually add the powdered sugar and vanilla extract, beating until fluffy.
5. **Assemble the Cake**:
   Spread a layer of frosting between the cake layers and cover the top and sides with the remaining frosting. Decorate with additional walnuts if desired.

Chocolate Mousse

Ingredients:

- 8 oz semisweet or bittersweet chocolate, chopped
- 1 cup heavy cream, plus 1/2 cup for whipping
- 2 tablespoons sugar
- 1 teaspoon vanilla extract
- 2 large egg yolks
- 1 tablespoon water

Instructions:

1. **Melt the Chocolate**:
   Melt the chocolate and water together in a heatproof bowl over simmering water (double boiler method), stirring until smooth. Let it cool slightly.
2. **Whip the Cream**:
   In a separate bowl, whip 1 cup of heavy cream and sugar to stiff peaks.
3. **Combine the Mixtures**:
   In a small saucepan, whisk the egg yolks. Gradually add the melted chocolate and vanilla extract to the yolks, stirring gently. Fold in the whipped cream until smooth.
4. **Chill**:
   Divide the mousse into serving glasses and chill for at least 2 hours before serving.

Cinnamon Rolls

Ingredients for the Dough:

- 3 1/4 cups all-purpose flour
- 1/4 cup sugar
- 1 packet active dry yeast
- 1 teaspoon salt
- 1/2 cup warm milk
- 1/4 cup unsalted butter, softened
- 2 large eggs

Ingredients for the Filling:

- 1/2 cup unsalted butter, softened
- 1 cup brown sugar
- 2 tablespoons ground cinnamon
- 1/2 cup chopped pecans or walnuts (optional)

Ingredients for the Glaze:

- 2 cups powdered sugar
- 1/4 cup cream cheese, softened
- 2 tablespoons unsalted butter, softened
- 1 teaspoon vanilla extract
- 1-2 tablespoons milk

Instructions:

1. **Make the Dough**:
   In a large bowl, combine the flour, sugar, yeast, and salt. Add the warm milk, butter, and eggs, and mix until the dough comes together. Knead the dough on a floured surface for 5-7 minutes, then cover and let it rise for 1 hour.
2. **Prepare the Filling**:
   In a bowl, mix the softened butter, brown sugar, and cinnamon. Roll the dough out on a floured surface into a large rectangle. Spread the cinnamon-sugar filling over the dough and sprinkle with nuts if using. Roll up the dough tightly and slice into 12 rolls.
3. **Bake the Rolls**:
   Place the rolls in a greased baking dish and let them rise for 30 minutes. Preheat the oven to 350°F (175°C) and bake the rolls for 20-25 minutes.
4. **Make the Glaze**:
   Mix the cream cheese, butter, powdered sugar, vanilla, and milk until smooth. Drizzle over the warm cinnamon rolls and serve.

Lemon Bars

Ingredients for the Crust:

- 1 1/2 cups all-purpose flour
- 1/4 cup powdered sugar
- 1/2 teaspoon salt
- 1/2 cup unsalted butter, softened

Ingredients for the Filling:

- 1 1/2 cups granulated sugar
- 1/4 cup all-purpose flour
- 1/2 teaspoon baking powder
- 4 large eggs
- 2/3 cup fresh lemon juice
- Powdered sugar for dusting

Instructions:

1. **Make the Crust**:
   Preheat the oven to 350°F (175°C). In a bowl, combine the flour, powdered sugar, and salt. Cut in the butter until the mixture forms a dough. Press the dough into the bottom of a greased 9x9-inch baking dish. Bake for 15-20 minutes, until golden.
2. **Make the Filling**:
   Whisk together the sugar, flour, baking powder, eggs, and lemon juice. Pour over the baked crust.
3. **Bake the Bars**:
   Bake for 25-30 minutes, or until the filling is set. Let cool completely, then dust with powdered sugar and cut into squares.

Peppermint Bark

Ingredients:

- 8 oz semisweet chocolate
- 8 oz white chocolate
- 1/2 teaspoon peppermint extract
- 1/2 cup crushed peppermint candies or candy canes

Instructions:

1. **Melt the Chocolate:**
   Melt the semisweet chocolate in a heatproof bowl over simmering water, stirring until smooth. Pour onto a parchment-lined baking sheet and spread into an even layer. Chill in the refrigerator for 15 minutes.
2. **Melt the White Chocolate:**
   Melt the white chocolate in the same manner and stir in the peppermint extract.
3. **Assemble the Bark:**
   Spread the white chocolate over the chilled semisweet chocolate. Sprinkle with crushed peppermint candies. Chill until firm, then break into pieces.

Fruitcake

Ingredients:

- 1 1/2 cups mixed dried fruits (raisins, currants, cranberries)
- 1/2 cup chopped candied ginger
- 1/2 cup chopped walnuts or pecans
- 1 cup orange juice
- 1 cup unsalted butter, softened
- 1 cup brown sugar
- 4 large eggs
- 2 1/2 cups all-purpose flour
- 1 1/2 teaspoons baking powder
- 1 teaspoon ground cinnamon
- 1/2 teaspoon ground cloves
- 1/2 teaspoon ground nutmeg
- 1/4 teaspoon salt
- 1/4 cup dark rum (optional)

Instructions:

1. **Prepare the Fruit**:
   Soak the dried fruits and candied ginger in orange juice for 2 hours.
2. **Make the Cake**:
   Preheat the oven to 325°F (165°C). Cream the butter and brown sugar together. Add the eggs one at a time, then stir in the soaked fruit and nuts. In a separate bowl, whisk together the dry ingredients and fold them into the wet mixture. Pour into a greased loaf pan.
3. **Bake**:
   Bake for 1 1/2-2 hours, until a toothpick comes out clean. Let cool completely before serving.

Molasses Cookies

Ingredients:

- 2 1/4 cups all-purpose flour
- 1 teaspoon baking soda
- 1/2 teaspoon salt
- 1 teaspoon ground ginger
- 1 teaspoon ground cinnamon
- 1/2 teaspoon ground cloves
- 1/2 cup unsalted butter, softened
- 1 cup granulated sugar
- 1 large egg
- 1/4 cup molasses
- Extra sugar for rolling

Instructions:

1. **Preheat the Oven**:
   Preheat your oven to 350°F (175°C). Line baking sheets with parchment paper.
2. **Make the Dough**:
   In a bowl, whisk together the flour, baking soda, salt, and spices. In another bowl, cream the butter and sugar until smooth. Add the egg and molasses, then gradually add the dry ingredients.
3. **Shape the Cookies**:
   Roll the dough into balls, then roll in sugar. Place on the baking sheets and bake for 8-10 minutes. Let cool before serving.

Cherry Clafoutis

Ingredients:

- 2 cups fresh or frozen cherries, pitted
- 1 tablespoon butter, for greasing
- 3/4 cup whole milk
- 3/4 cup heavy cream
- 1/4 cup granulated sugar
- 1 teaspoon vanilla extract
- 3 large eggs
- 1/2 cup all-purpose flour
- 1/4 teaspoon salt

Instructions:

1. **Preheat the Oven**:
   Preheat your oven to 350°F (175°C). Grease a pie dish with butter.
2. **Prepare the Cherries**:
   Place the cherries in the bottom of the dish.
3. **Make the Batter**:
   In a bowl, whisk together the milk, cream, sugar, vanilla, eggs, flour, and salt. Pour over the cherries.
4. **Bake**:
   Bake for 40-45 minutes, or until the clafoutis is golden and puffed. Serve warm.

Chocolate-Dipped Strawberries

Ingredients:

- 1 lb (450g) fresh strawberries, washed and dried (leaving the stems on)
- 8 oz (225g) semi-sweet or dark chocolate, chopped (or use chocolate chips)
- 4 oz (115g) white chocolate (optional, for drizzling)
- 1 teaspoon vegetable oil or coconut oil (optional, for smooth melting)

Instructions:

1. **Prep the Strawberries:**
   Wash the strawberries and carefully pat them dry with a paper towel. Ensure the strawberries are completely dry to prevent the chocolate from seizing.
2. **Melt the Chocolate:**
   In a heatproof bowl, melt the semi-sweet or dark chocolate. You can do this in a microwave in 20-second intervals, stirring in between, or use a double boiler over simmering water until smooth. If you'd like a smoother texture, add a teaspoon of vegetable oil or coconut oil.
3. **Dip the Strawberries:**
   Hold each strawberry by the stem and dip it into the melted chocolate, covering about two-thirds of the strawberry. Gently shake off any excess chocolate.
4. **Cool the Strawberries:**
   Place the dipped strawberries on a parchment-lined baking sheet. Let the chocolate harden at room temperature, or speed up the process by refrigerating them for about 30 minutes.
5. **Optional White Chocolate Drizzle:**
   To add a decorative touch, melt the white chocolate in the same way as the dark chocolate. Once melted, drizzle it over the chocolate-dipped strawberries using a spoon or fork.
6. **Serve:**
   Once the chocolate is set, the strawberries are ready to serve. Enjoy these delicious treats as a dessert or gift!

Raisin Pudding Cake

Ingredients for the Cake:

- 1 cup all-purpose flour
- 3/4 cup granulated sugar
- 1/2 teaspoon baking powder
- 1/2 teaspoon salt
- 1 teaspoon ground cinnamon
- 1/2 teaspoon ground nutmeg
- 1/2 cup milk
- 1/4 cup unsalted butter, melted
- 1 large egg
- 1 cup raisins

Ingredients for the Sauce:

- 1 1/2 cups water
- 1 cup brown sugar, packed
- 1/2 teaspoon vanilla extract

Instructions:

1. **Preheat the Oven:**
   Preheat your oven to 350°F (175°C). Grease a 9-inch baking dish or a similar size casserole dish.
2. **Prepare the Cake Batter:**
   In a medium bowl, combine the flour, sugar, baking powder, salt, cinnamon, and nutmeg. In a separate bowl, whisk together the milk, melted butter, and egg. Add the wet ingredients to the dry ingredients and stir until combined. Fold in the raisins.
3. **Prepare the Sauce:**
   In a saucepan, bring the water and brown sugar to a boil, stirring occasionally until the sugar dissolves. Remove from heat and stir in the vanilla extract.
4. **Assemble the Cake:**
   Pour the cake batter into the prepared baking dish. Carefully pour the hot sugar syrup over the batter. Do not stir—it will create a saucy bottom layer during baking.
5. **Bake:**
   Bake for 35-40 minutes, or until the top is golden and the cake has set. The sauce will bubble up from the bottom during baking, creating a rich, caramel-like base.
6. **Serve:**
   Let the pudding cake cool for a few minutes before serving. Serve warm, optionally with a scoop of vanilla ice cream or a dollop of whipped cream.

Tiramisu

Ingredients:

- 6 large egg yolks
- 3/4 cup granulated sugar
- 1 cup mascarpone cheese
- 1 1/2 cups heavy cream
- 2 cups strong brewed coffee, cooled
- 1/4 cup coffee liqueur (optional)
- 2 packs of ladyfingers
- Cocoa powder, for dusting
- Dark chocolate shavings (optional)

Instructions:

1. **Make the Cream**:
   In a bowl, whisk the egg yolks and sugar together until smooth. Add mascarpone cheese and whisk until combined. In a separate bowl, whip the heavy cream until stiff peaks form. Gently fold the whipped cream into the mascarpone mixture.
2. **Soak the Ladyfingers**:
   Quickly dip the ladyfingers into the coffee and coffee liqueur mixture (do not soak them too long, as they will become soggy).
3. **Assemble the Tiramisu**:
   Layer the soaked ladyfingers in a 9x13-inch dish. Spread half of the mascarpone mixture on top. Repeat with another layer of soaked ladyfingers and mascarpone mixture.
4. **Chill and Serve**:
   Cover and refrigerate for at least 4 hours, preferably overnight. Before serving, dust with cocoa powder and top with chocolate shavings.

Coconut Cream Pie

Ingredients for the Crust:

- 1 1/2 cups graham cracker crumbs
- 1/4 cup sugar
- 1/2 cup unsalted butter, melted

Ingredients for the Filling:

- 1 can (14 oz) coconut milk
- 1 cup heavy cream
- 3/4 cup granulated sugar
- 1/4 cup cornstarch
- 1/2 teaspoon vanilla extract
- 1/2 cup sweetened shredded coconut

Ingredients for the Topping:

- 1 cup heavy cream
- 2 tablespoons powdered sugar
- 1/2 teaspoon vanilla extract
- Toasted coconut flakes for garnish

Instructions:

1. **Make the Crust**:
   Preheat the oven to 350°F (175°C). Mix graham cracker crumbs, sugar, and melted butter until well combined. Press into the bottom of a pie dish. Bake for 10 minutes and set aside to cool.
2. **Make the Filling**:
   In a saucepan, combine coconut milk, heavy cream, sugar, and cornstarch. Cook over medium heat, whisking constantly until the mixture thickens, about 5-7 minutes. Remove from heat and stir in vanilla extract and shredded coconut.
3. **Assemble the Pie**:
   Pour the filling into the cooled pie crust. Refrigerate for at least 4 hours.
4. **Make the Topping**:
   Whip the heavy cream, powdered sugar, and vanilla extract until stiff peaks form. Spread over the cooled pie and garnish with toasted coconut flakes.

Pavlova with Berries

Ingredients:

- 4 large egg whites
- 1 cup granulated sugar
- 1 teaspoon vanilla extract
- 1 teaspoon white vinegar
- 1/2 teaspoon cornstarch
- 1 cup heavy cream
- 1 tablespoon powdered sugar
- Mixed fresh berries (strawberries, blueberries, raspberries)

Instructions:

1. **Make the Meringue**:
   Preheat the oven to 250°F (120°C). Whisk the egg whites until stiff peaks form. Gradually add the sugar, 1 tablespoon at a time, continuing to whisk until glossy and thick. Fold in vanilla extract, vinegar, and cornstarch.
2. **Shape the Pavlova**:
   Spoon the meringue onto a parchment-lined baking sheet, shaping it into a round nest with a slight well in the center.
3. **Bake**:
   Bake for 1 hour, then turn off the oven and let the meringue cool completely in the oven with the door slightly ajar.
4. **Whip the Cream**:
   Whip the heavy cream and powdered sugar until stiff peaks form. Spoon the whipped cream onto the cooled meringue and top with fresh berries.

Baked Alaska

Ingredients:

- 1/2 gallon ice cream (flavor of choice)
- 1 pound cake (sponge or angel food cake)
- 6 large egg whites
- 1 cup granulated sugar
- 1/2 teaspoon vanilla extract

Instructions:

1. **Prepare the Base**:
   Cut the pound cake into slices and arrange them in a round baking dish. Pack the ice cream on top, smoothing it into an even layer. Freeze the cake and ice cream base until firm, about 2 hours.
2. **Make the Meringue**:
   Whisk the egg whites until stiff peaks form. Gradually add sugar and vanilla, continuing to whisk until glossy.
3. **Assemble and Bake**:
   Preheat the oven to 500°F (260°C). Cover the frozen cake and ice cream with meringue, making sure to seal the edges. Bake for 3-5 minutes until the meringue is golden brown. Serve immediately.

Red Velvet Cake

Ingredients for the Cake:

- 2 1/2 cups all-purpose flour
- 1 1/2 teaspoons baking soda
- 1 teaspoon cocoa powder
- 1 teaspoon salt
- 1 cup vegetable oil
- 1 1/2 cups granulated sugar
- 2 large eggs
- 1 teaspoon vanilla extract
- 1 cup buttermilk
- 1 tablespoon red food coloring
- 1 teaspoon white vinegar

Ingredients for the Cream Cheese Frosting:

- 8 oz cream cheese, softened
- 1/2 cup unsalted butter, softened
- 4 cups powdered sugar
- 1 teaspoon vanilla extract

Instructions:

1. **Make the Cake**:
   Preheat the oven to 350°F (175°C). Grease and flour two 9-inch round cake pans. Mix the dry ingredients in one bowl. In another bowl, whisk the oil, sugar, eggs, vanilla, buttermilk, food coloring, and vinegar. Gradually add the dry ingredients to the wet ingredients.
2. **Bake the Cake**:
   Divide the batter between the two pans and bake for 25-30 minutes, or until a toothpick comes out clean. Let cool completely.
3. **Make the Frosting**:
   Beat the cream cheese and butter until smooth. Gradually add the powdered sugar and vanilla extract. Frost the cooled cakes and serve.

Marzipan Cookies

Ingredients:

- 1 1/2 cups marzipan
- 1/4 cup powdered sugar
- 1 teaspoon vanilla extract
- 1 egg white, beaten (for brushing)

Instructions:

1. **Prepare the Dough**:
   Mix the marzipan, powdered sugar, and vanilla extract until smooth. Shape the mixture into small cookie shapes (balls or discs).
2. **Bake**:
   Preheat the oven to 350°F (175°C). Brush the cookies with the beaten egg white and bake for 10-12 minutes until golden. Let cool before serving.

Ricotta Cheesecake

Ingredients:

- 1 1/2 pounds ricotta cheese
- 1 cup granulated sugar
- 3 large eggs
- 1 teaspoon vanilla extract
- 1 tablespoon lemon zest
- 1/4 cup all-purpose flour
- 1/4 teaspoon salt

Instructions:

1. **Make the Filling**:
   Preheat the oven to 350°F (175°C). Beat the ricotta cheese with the sugar until smooth. Add the eggs one at a time, then stir in vanilla, lemon zest, flour, and salt.
2. **Bake**:
   Pour the batter into a greased springform pan and bake for 40-45 minutes until set. Let cool and refrigerate before serving.

Sweet Potato Pie

Ingredients for the Filling:

- 2 cups mashed sweet potatoes
- 1 cup granulated sugar
- 1 teaspoon ground cinnamon
- 1/2 teaspoon ground nutmeg
- 1/4 teaspoon ground ginger
- 1/4 teaspoon salt
- 3/4 cup evaporated milk
- 2 large eggs
- 1 teaspoon vanilla extract

Ingredients for the Crust:

- 1 pre-made pie crust

Instructions:

1. **Make the Filling**:
   Preheat the oven to 350°F (175°C). In a bowl, mix the sweet potatoes, sugar, spices, salt, evaporated milk, eggs, and vanilla until smooth.
2. **Assemble and Bake**:
   Pour the filling into the pie crust. Bake for 45-50 minutes until set. Let cool before serving.

S'mores Brownies

Ingredients:

- 1 box brownie mix
- 1 cup graham cracker crumbs
- 1 cup mini marshmallows
- 1 cup chocolate chips

Instructions:

1. **Prepare the Brownies**:
   Prepare the brownie mix according to package instructions, and pour it into a greased baking pan.
2. **Add the S'mores Topping**:
   Layer graham cracker crumbs, marshmallows, and chocolate chips on top of the brownie batter.
3. **Bake**:
   Bake according to the package instructions, adding 5-10 extra minutes to ensure the marshmallows are toasted. Let cool and slice.

Fudge (Chocolate, Peanut Butter, or Maple)

Ingredients for Chocolate Fudge:

- 2 cups chocolate chips
- 1/2 cup sweetened condensed milk
- 1 teaspoon vanilla extract

Instructions:

1. **Make the Fudge**:
   Melt the chocolate chips with the sweetened condensed milk in a saucepan over low heat. Stir in vanilla extract.
2. **Set the Fudge**:
   Pour into a greased dish and refrigerate for 2 hours or until set. Cut into squares.

Meringue Kisses

Ingredients:

- 4 large egg whites
- 1 cup granulated sugar
- 1 teaspoon vanilla extract
- 1/2 teaspoon lemon juice or cream of tartar (optional)

Instructions:

1. **Preheat the Oven**:
   Preheat your oven to 200°F (93°C). Line a baking sheet with parchment paper.
2. **Whip the Egg Whites**:
   Beat the egg whites with an electric mixer on medium speed until soft peaks form. Add the lemon juice or cream of tartar to stabilize the meringue, then gradually add the sugar while continuing to beat until stiff, glossy peaks form.
3. **Pipe the Meringues**:
   Spoon the meringue into a piping bag fitted with a star or plain nozzle. Pipe small mounds or kisses onto the prepared baking sheet.
4. **Bake**:
   Bake for 1 to 1.5 hours, or until the meringues are dry and crisp. Turn off the oven and let them cool completely in the oven with the door slightly ajar.

Peach Cobbler

Ingredients:

- 4 cups fresh or frozen peaches, sliced
- 1/2 cup granulated sugar
- 1 tablespoon cornstarch
- 1 teaspoon vanilla extract
- 1 tablespoon lemon juice
- 1 cup all-purpose flour
- 1/2 cup granulated sugar (for the batter)
- 1 teaspoon baking powder
- 1/4 teaspoon salt
- 1/2 cup milk
- 1/4 cup unsalted butter, melted

Instructions:

1. **Prepare the Peaches**:
   Preheat the oven to 375°F (190°C). In a bowl, toss the peaches with sugar, cornstarch, vanilla extract, and lemon juice. Pour the peach mixture into a greased 9x9-inch baking dish.
2. **Make the Batter**:
   In a separate bowl, whisk together flour, sugar, baking powder, and salt. Stir in the milk and melted butter until a thick batter forms.
3. **Assemble and Bake**:
   Dollop the batter over the peaches, spreading it out as best as you can. Bake for 40-45 minutes, until the topping is golden brown and the peaches are bubbling.

Black Forest Cake

Ingredients for the Cake:

- 1 1/2 cups all-purpose flour
- 1 cup granulated sugar
- 1/2 cup unsweetened cocoa powder
- 1 teaspoon baking powder
- 1/2 teaspoon baking soda
- 1/2 teaspoon salt
- 2 large eggs
- 1 cup whole milk
- 1/2 cup vegetable oil
- 1 teaspoon vanilla extract
- 1 cup boiling water

Ingredients for the Filling:

- 1 jar (14 oz) maraschino cherries, drained
- 1 cup heavy whipping cream
- 1/4 cup powdered sugar
- 1 teaspoon vanilla extract

Instructions:

1. **Make the Cake**:
   Preheat the oven to 350°F (175°C). Grease and flour two 9-inch round cake pans. In a large bowl, mix the dry ingredients. Add eggs, milk, oil, and vanilla, then mix until smooth. Gradually add the boiling water and mix until the batter is thin.
2. **Bake the Cake**:
   Pour the batter evenly into the prepared pans. Bake for 30-35 minutes, or until a toothpick inserted comes out clean. Let the cakes cool.
3. **Assemble the Cake**:
   Whip the heavy cream with powdered sugar and vanilla until stiff peaks form. Slice each cake in half horizontally. Layer the cake with whipped cream and cherries between each layer. Frost the top and sides with the remaining whipped cream and top with more cherries.

Banoffee Pie

Ingredients for the Crust:

- 1 1/2 cups graham cracker crumbs
- 1/4 cup sugar
- 1/2 cup unsalted butter, melted

Ingredients for the Filling:

- 2 ripe bananas
- 1 can (14 oz) sweetened condensed milk
- 1/4 cup unsalted butter
- 1 tablespoon brown sugar

Ingredients for the Topping:

- 1 cup heavy cream
- 2 tablespoons powdered sugar
- 1/2 teaspoon vanilla extract

Instructions:

1. **Make the Crust**:
   Preheat the oven to 350°F (175°C). Mix the graham cracker crumbs, sugar, and melted butter. Press into the bottom of a pie dish and bake for 8-10 minutes. Let cool.
2. **Make the Toffee Filling**:
   In a saucepan, combine sweetened condensed milk, butter, and brown sugar. Heat over medium heat, stirring constantly, until it thickens (about 10 minutes). Let cool slightly.
3. **Assemble the Pie**:
   Spread the toffee mixture over the cooled crust. Slice the bananas and arrange them over the toffee. Whip the heavy cream with powdered sugar and vanilla until stiff peaks form, then spread over the bananas.

Chocolate Fondue

Ingredients:

- 8 oz semisweet or dark chocolate, chopped
- 1 cup heavy cream
- 1 tablespoon butter
- 1 teaspoon vanilla extract

Instructions:

1. **Melt the Chocolate**:
   In a heatproof bowl, combine the chocolate, cream, and butter. Place the bowl over a pot of simmering water and stir until melted and smooth. Stir in vanilla extract.
2. **Serve**:
   Serve the fondue in a fondue pot with dippable items like strawberries, marshmallows, or pieces of cake.

Fruit Sorbet

Ingredients:

- 4 cups fresh fruit (e.g., mango, strawberries, or raspberries)
- 1/2 cup sugar (adjust to sweetness)
- 1/2 cup water
- 1 tablespoon lemon juice

Instructions:

1. **Prepare the Fruit**:
   Puree the fruit in a blender or food processor until smooth. Add sugar, water, and lemon juice, blending again.
2. **Freeze the Sorbet**:
   Pour the mixture into a shallow pan and freeze for at least 4 hours, scraping every 30 minutes with a fork to create a fluffy texture.

Churros with Chocolate Sauce

Ingredients for the Churros:

- 1 cup water
- 1/4 cup unsalted butter
- 1 tablespoon sugar
- 1/2 teaspoon salt
- 1 cup all-purpose flour
- 3 large eggs
- Vegetable oil for frying
- Cinnamon sugar for coating

Ingredients for the Chocolate Sauce:

- 1/2 cup heavy cream
- 4 oz semisweet chocolate, chopped

Instructions:

1. **Make the Churros**:
   In a saucepan, heat water, butter, sugar, and salt until it boils. Remove from heat and stir in flour until a dough forms. Let it cool slightly, then beat in eggs one at a time.
2. **Fry the Churros**:
   Heat oil in a deep pan. Spoon the dough into a piping bag fitted with a star nozzle. Pipe strips of dough into the hot oil and fry until golden brown. Drain on paper towels and coat in cinnamon sugar.
3. **Make the Chocolate Sauce**:
   Heat heavy cream in a saucepan until simmering. Pour over chopped chocolate and stir until smooth. Serve with churros.

Cranberry Cheesecake Bars

Ingredients for the Crust:

- 1 1/2 cups graham cracker crumbs
- 1/4 cup granulated sugar
- 1/4 cup unsalted butter, melted

Ingredients for the Filling:

- 16 oz cream cheese, softened
- 1 cup granulated sugar
- 2 large eggs
- 1 teaspoon vanilla extract
- 1 cup fresh or frozen cranberries

Instructions:

1. **Make the Crust**:
   Preheat the oven to 350°F (175°C). Mix the graham cracker crumbs, sugar, and butter. Press into the bottom of a baking dish and bake for 8 minutes. Let cool.
2. **Make the Filling**:
   Beat the cream cheese with sugar until smooth. Add eggs and vanilla, beating until combined. Gently fold in the cranberries.
3. **Bake**:
   Pour the filling over the crust and bake for 30-35 minutes, or until set. Let cool before cutting into bars.

Chocolate-Covered Pretzels

Ingredients:

- 1 bag pretzel rods or mini pretzels
- 8 oz semisweet chocolate or white chocolate, melted
- Sprinkles or crushed nuts (optional)

Instructions:

1. **Melt the Chocolate:**
   Melt the chocolate in a microwave-safe bowl or over a double boiler.
2. **Dip the Pretzels:**
   Dip the pretzels halfway into the melted chocolate and place them on parchment paper. Sprinkle with toppings, if desired.
3. **Let Set:**
   Allow the chocolate to set at room temperature or refrigerate to speed up the process.

Key Lime Pie

Ingredients for the Crust:

- 1 1/2 cups graham cracker crumbs
- 1/4 cup sugar
- 1/2 cup unsalted butter, melted

Ingredients for the Filling:

- 1 can (14 oz) sweetened condensed milk
- 1/2 cup key lime juice (fresh or bottled)
- 3 large egg yolks

Ingredients for the Topping:

- 1 cup heavy whipping cream
- 2 tablespoons powdered sugar
- 1/2 teaspoon vanilla extract

Instructions:

1. **Make the Crust**:
   Preheat the oven to 350°F (175°C). Mix graham cracker crumbs, sugar, and melted butter, then press into the bottom of a pie pan. Bake for 8-10 minutes and let cool.
2. **Make the Filling**:
   Whisk together sweetened condensed milk, lime juice, and egg yolks. Pour into the cooled crust and bake for 15 minutes.
3. **Make the Topping**:
   Whip the heavy cream with powdered sugar and vanilla until stiff peaks form. Spread over the cooled pie.

Rugelach

Ingredients for the Dough:

- 2 cups all-purpose flour
- 1/4 teaspoon salt
- 1 cup unsalted butter, softened
- 8 oz cream cheese, softened
- 1/4 cup granulated sugar
- 1 teaspoon vanilla extract

Ingredients for the Filling:

- 1/4 cup granulated sugar
- 1 teaspoon ground cinnamon
- 1/2 cup finely chopped walnuts or pecans
- 1/4 cup raisins or currants
- 1/4 cup apricot or raspberry jam

Ingredients for the Topping:

- 1/4 cup granulated sugar
- 1 teaspoon ground cinnamon

Instructions:

1. **Make the Dough**:
   In a large bowl, mix the flour and salt. Add the butter, cream cheese, sugar, and vanilla, then blend until a dough forms. Wrap the dough in plastic wrap and refrigerate for at least 1 hour.
2. **Prepare the Filling**:
   In a small bowl, combine the sugar, cinnamon, nuts, and raisins.
3. **Assemble the Rugelach**:
   Roll out the dough into a circle about 1/8 inch thick. Spread a thin layer of jam over the dough. Sprinkle the filling evenly on top, then cut the dough into 8 wedges. Roll each wedge tightly from the wider edge.
4. **Bake**:
   Place the cookies on a lined baking sheet. Mix the sugar and cinnamon for the topping, and sprinkle over the cookies. Bake at 350°F (175°C) for 20-25 minutes, until golden brown.

Baked Apple Dumplings

Ingredients:

- 4 medium apples (peeled, cored, and halved)
- 1/4 cup unsalted butter, melted
- 1/4 cup brown sugar
- 1 teaspoon ground cinnamon
- 1/4 teaspoon ground nutmeg
- 1 package refrigerated crescent roll dough
- 1 cup ginger ale or lemon-lime soda

Instructions:

1. **Prepare the Apples**:
   Preheat the oven to 350°F (175°C). Arrange the apple halves in a greased baking dish.
2. **Make the Filling**:
   In a small bowl, mix the brown sugar, cinnamon, and nutmeg. Place a little of this mixture inside the hollow of each apple half.
3. **Wrap the Apples**:
   Unroll the crescent roll dough and wrap each apple half in one triangle of dough, pinching the seams closed.
4. **Bake**:
   Pour the melted butter over the apples and drizzle the remaining brown sugar mixture over the top. Pour the ginger ale or soda around the apples and bake for 35-40 minutes, until golden brown and the apples are tender.

Cinnamon Sugar Donuts

Ingredients:

- 1 cup all-purpose flour
- 1/2 cup granulated sugar
- 1 1/2 teaspoons baking powder
- 1/4 teaspoon salt
- 1/4 teaspoon ground cinnamon
- 1/2 cup milk
- 2 large eggs
- 2 tablespoons unsalted butter, melted
- 1 teaspoon vanilla extract

Ingredients for the Coating:

- 1/2 cup granulated sugar
- 1 tablespoon ground cinnamon

Instructions:

1. **Prepare the Donuts**:
   Preheat the oven to 350°F (175°C). Grease a donut pan. In a bowl, whisk together flour, sugar, baking powder, salt, and cinnamon. In another bowl, whisk together milk, eggs, melted butter, and vanilla.
2. **Make the Donut Batter**:
   Add the wet ingredients to the dry ingredients and mix until just combined. Spoon the batter into the donut pan, filling each cavity about 2/3 full.
3. **Bake**:
   Bake for 10-12 minutes or until a toothpick comes out clean. Let the donuts cool for a few minutes.
4. **Coat the Donuts**:
   Mix the cinnamon and sugar together. While the donuts are still warm, dip them into the cinnamon sugar mixture, coating evenly.

Sticky Toffee Pudding

Ingredients for the Pudding:

- 1 cup dates, pitted and chopped
- 1 cup boiling water
- 1/2 teaspoon baking soda
- 1/4 cup unsalted butter, softened
- 1/2 cup granulated sugar
- 1 large egg
- 1 teaspoon vanilla extract
- 1 cup all-purpose flour
- 1 teaspoon baking powder

Ingredients for the Sauce:

- 1/2 cup unsalted butter
- 1/2 cup brown sugar
- 1/2 cup heavy cream
- 1 teaspoon vanilla extract

Instructions:

1. **Make the Pudding**:
   Preheat the oven to 350°F (175°C). In a bowl, pour boiling water over the dates and stir in the baking soda. Let sit for 10 minutes, then blend until smooth.
2. **Prepare the Batter**:
   In a separate bowl, cream the butter and sugar together. Add the egg and vanilla extract and beat well. Mix in the flour and baking powder, then fold in the date mixture.
3. **Bake**:
   Pour the batter into a greased baking dish and bake for 30-35 minutes, or until a toothpick inserted comes out clean.
4. **Make the Sauce**:
   In a saucepan, melt the butter with brown sugar and cream. Bring to a simmer, stirring constantly. Let it cook for 5 minutes until thickened, then remove from heat and stir in vanilla.
5. **Serve**:
   Serve the warm pudding with the toffee sauce poured over the top.

Chocolate Lava Cakes

Ingredients:

- 1/2 cup unsalted butter
- 8 oz semisweet or bittersweet chocolate
- 2 eggs
- 2 egg yolks
- 1/4 cup granulated sugar
- 1/4 teaspoon vanilla extract
- 1/4 teaspoon salt
- 1/4 cup all-purpose flour

Instructions:

1. **Prepare the Cakes**:
   Preheat the oven to 425°F (220°C). Grease and flour 4 ramekins. Melt the butter and chocolate together in a microwave or over a double boiler. Let cool slightly.
2. **Make the Batter**:
   Whisk together the eggs, egg yolks, sugar, vanilla, and salt. Add the melted chocolate mixture and flour and whisk until smooth.
3. **Bake**:
   Divide the batter evenly among the ramekins. Bake for 12-14 minutes, until the edges are set but the center is still soft. Let the cakes cool for a minute, then invert them onto plates and serve.

Lemon Meringue Pie

Ingredients for the Crust:

- 1 1/2 cups graham cracker crumbs
- 1/4 cup granulated sugar
- 1/2 cup unsalted butter, melted

Ingredients for the Lemon Filling:

- 1 cup granulated sugar
- 2 tablespoons cornstarch
- 1 1/2 cups water
- 3 large egg yolks
- 1/2 cup freshly squeezed lemon juice
- 2 teaspoons lemon zest
- 1 tablespoon unsalted butter

Ingredients for the Meringue:

- 3 large egg whites
- 1/4 teaspoon cream of tartar
- 1/4 cup granulated sugar

Instructions:

1. **Make the Crust**:
   Preheat the oven to 350°F (175°C). Mix graham cracker crumbs, sugar, and melted butter. Press into the bottom of a pie dish and bake for 8-10 minutes. Let cool.
2. **Prepare the Lemon Filling**:
   In a saucepan, combine sugar and cornstarch. Gradually add water and cook over medium heat until it thickens. In a separate bowl, whisk the egg yolks, then temper them by adding a small amount of the hot mixture. Return the egg yolk mixture to the saucepan and cook for another 2-3 minutes. Stir in lemon juice, zest, and butter.
3. **Make the Meringue**:
   Whip egg whites and cream of tartar until soft peaks form. Gradually add sugar and continue whipping until stiff peaks form.
4. **Assemble the Pie**:
   Pour the lemon filling into the cooled crust. Spread the meringue over the filling, making sure it touches the edges of the crust. Bake for 10-12 minutes, until the meringue is golden.

Almond Biscotti

Ingredients:

- 1 3/4 cups all-purpose flour
- 1 cup granulated sugar
- 1 teaspoon baking powder
- 1/2 teaspoon salt
- 2 large eggs
- 1 teaspoon vanilla extract
- 1 teaspoon almond extract
- 1 cup whole almonds, toasted

Instructions:

1. **Prepare the Dough**:
   Preheat the oven to 350°F (175°C). In a bowl, mix the flour, sugar, baking powder, and salt. In another bowl, whisk the eggs, vanilla, and almond extracts. Add the wet ingredients to the dry ingredients and mix until just combined. Fold in the toasted almonds.
2. **Shape and Bake**:
   Divide the dough in half and form two logs. Place them on a baking sheet and bake for 25 minutes. Let them cool for 10 minutes, then slice them diagonally.
3. **Second Bake**:
   Lay the slices cut-side down on the baking sheet and bake for another 10 minutes, flipping halfway through. Let cool completely.

Chantilly Cream-Filled Profiteroles

Ingredients for the Pâte à Choux (Choux Pastry):

- 1/2 cup unsalted butter
- 1 cup water
- 1 cup all-purpose flour
- 1/4 teaspoon salt
- 1 teaspoon granulated sugar
- 4 large eggs

Ingredients for the Chantilly Cream:

- 1 cup heavy whipping cream
- 1/4 cup powdered sugar
- 1 teaspoon vanilla extract

Instructions:

1. **Prepare the Pâte à Choux**:
   Preheat your oven to 400°F (200°C). Line a baking sheet with parchment paper. In a saucepan, melt butter with water, salt, and sugar over medium heat. Once the butter has melted, bring the mixture to a boil. Quickly add the flour, stirring constantly until the mixture forms a ball and pulls away from the sides of the pan.
2. **Form the Choux Pastry**:
   Remove the dough from the heat and let it cool for a few minutes. Add the eggs one at a time, mixing thoroughly after each addition until the dough is smooth and shiny. Spoon the dough into a piping bag or a plastic bag with the tip cut off.
3. **Bake the Profiteroles**:
   Pipe small mounds (about 1 1/2 inches) onto the baking sheet, spacing them about 2 inches apart. Bake for 20-25 minutes, or until golden brown and puffed up. Let cool on a wire rack.
4. **Make the Chantilly Cream**:
   Whisk the heavy cream, powdered sugar, and vanilla extract together in a large bowl until soft peaks form.
5. **Fill the Profiteroles**:
   Once the profiteroles have cooled, cut a small hole in the bottom of each one and pipe the Chantilly cream into the center.

Berry Crumble

Ingredients for the Fruit Filling:

- 4 cups mixed berries (such as strawberries, raspberries, blueberries, and blackberries)
- 1/4 cup granulated sugar
- 1 tablespoon cornstarch
- 1 tablespoon lemon juice
- 1/2 teaspoon vanilla extract

Ingredients for the Crumble Topping:

- 3/4 cup all-purpose flour
- 1/2 cup rolled oats
- 1/3 cup brown sugar
- 1/4 teaspoon ground cinnamon
- 1/4 teaspoon salt
- 1/2 cup unsalted butter, cold and cubed

Instructions:

1. **Prepare the Fruit Filling:**
   Preheat the oven to 375°F (190°C). In a large bowl, combine the berries, sugar, cornstarch, lemon juice, and vanilla. Stir gently to coat the berries. Transfer the mixture into a greased 9x9-inch baking dish.
2. **Make the Crumble Topping:**
   In a separate bowl, mix together the flour, oats, brown sugar, cinnamon, and salt. Add the cold cubed butter and use your fingers or a pastry cutter to work the butter into the dry ingredients until the mixture resembles coarse crumbs.
3. **Assemble and Bake:**
   Sprinkle the crumble topping evenly over the berry mixture. Bake for 35-40 minutes, or until the topping is golden brown and the filling is bubbling. Serve warm, optionally with a scoop of vanilla ice cream or whipped cream.

Chocolate-Coconut Macaroons

Ingredients:

- 2 1/2 cups sweetened shredded coconut
- 1/2 cup semi-sweet chocolate chips
- 1/4 cup granulated sugar
- 1/4 cup all-purpose flour
- 2 large egg whites
- 1 teaspoon vanilla extract
- 1/4 teaspoon salt

Instructions:

1. **Prepare the Macaroon Mixture**:
   Preheat the oven to 350°F (175°C). Line a baking sheet with parchment paper. In a large bowl, combine the coconut, sugar, flour, egg whites, vanilla, and salt. Stir until well combined.
2. **Form the Macaroons**:
   Use a spoon or cookie scoop to form small mounds of the mixture and place them on the prepared baking sheet, spacing them about 2 inches apart.
3. **Bake**:
   Bake for 12-15 minutes, or until the edges of the macaroons are golden brown.
4. **Dip in Chocolate (Optional)**:
   In a microwave-safe bowl, melt the chocolate chips in 30-second intervals, stirring between each, until smooth. Once the macaroons are cool, dip the bottoms of each one into the melted chocolate and let them set on parchment paper.

Peach Melba

Ingredients:

- 4 ripe peaches, peeled, pitted, and halved
- 1/2 cup granulated sugar
- 1/4 cup water
- 1 teaspoon lemon juice
- 1 cup raspberry puree (or fresh raspberries)
- 2 cups vanilla ice cream
- Fresh raspberries and mint for garnish

Instructions:

1. **Prepare the Peaches**:
   In a saucepan, combine the sugar, water, and lemon juice. Bring to a simmer and stir until the sugar dissolves. Add the peach halves to the saucepan and simmer for about 5-8 minutes, until the peaches are tender but still hold their shape. Remove from the syrup and set aside.
2. **Make the Raspberry Sauce**:
   In a blender or food processor, blend the raspberries until smooth. Strain through a fine sieve to remove the seeds, and set the raspberry puree aside.
3. **Assemble the Peach Melba**:
   Place two peach halves on each serving dish. Spoon a scoop of vanilla ice cream in the center of each peach. Drizzle with raspberry sauce.
4. **Garnish and Serve**:
   Garnish with fresh raspberries and mint leaves. Serve immediately.

www.ingramcontent.com/pod-product-compliance
Lightning Source LLC
LaVergne TN
LVHW081325060526
838201LV00055B/2463